Raising the Roof
WNBA Action on the Court and Behind the Scenes

Jennifer Blake

SCHOLASTIC INC.
New York Toronto London Auckland Sydney
Mexico City New Delhi Hong Kong Buenos Aires

**Cover photo
Khue Bui, Associated Press, AP**

2   3   4   5   6   7   8   9   10   23   10 09 08 07 06 05 04 03

Contents

Introduction 4

Val Ackerman, WNBA President 6

*Time-out with Teresa Weatherspoon
of the New York Liberty* 10

Carolyn Peck, General Manager and
Head Coach of the Orlando Miracle 12

*Time-out with Chamique Holdsclaw
of the Washington Mystics* 16

Lisa White, Trainer for the New York Liberty . . 18

*Time-out with Ticha Penicheiro
of the Sacramento Monarchs* 22

Patty Broderick, Referee 24

*Time-out with Sheryl Swoopes
of the Houston Comets* 28

Alicia Parker, Director of Security 30

*Time-out with Nikki McCray
of the Indiana Fever* 34

Kristie Ackert, Sports Reporter 36

Introduction

The 1996–1997 season of the National Basketball Association (NBA) was ending. A new TV ad appeared. The commercial began with men playing basketball. This was nothing new.

But wait. Suddenly, women players came on the screen. Women ran onto the court. Women made fantastic shots. Women shouted out: "We Got Next!"

This *was* something new. Women called the court for the next game. And that next game was important. It was the first game of the Women's National Basketball Association (WNBA).

The WNBA is a league of professional women's basketball teams. Eight teams began playing. And more than 50 million people watched.

Today, the WNBA has grown from eight teams to 16. Players like Teresa Weatherspoon and Sheryl Swoopes thrill the crowds.

What does it mean that women have their

own league? In the early 1990s, there was no pro basketball league in the United States for women. Women had to leave the country to play pro ball.

Today, American girls can have hoop dreams. And those dreams can come true.

The WNBA made **opportunities** for female athletes. And it also made other opportunities for women.

Read on to find out what women are doing to make the WNBA a success.

Val Ackerman, WNBA President

"If there's one word that describes me best," says WNBA president Val Ackerman, "it's probably **pioneer**."

Ackerman is a true pioneer. She had the idea for the WNBA. She's known as "the first lady of women's basketball." But it took a lot of work.

"Sports are probably in my genes," she says. Ackerman's father and grandfather were athletic directors. They told Ackerman to follow her dreams.

Back then, there weren't many opportunities for girls. "My school didn't have any sports for girls. My only option was to be a cheerleader," she says. Ackerman didn't make the squad.

In college, Ackerman got to play basketball. But there wasn't much money for women's sports. The team had only one scholarship.

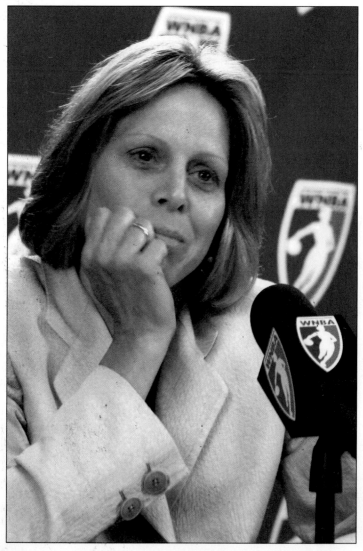

© AP Photo/Don Frazier

WNBA president Val Ackerman. She's answering questions before the 2000 All-Star Game in Orlando, Florida.

Ackerman got the scholarship. But she had to split it with her roommate.

Not many people were interested in the women's games. "We played in front of small crowds," she says. And the team didn't do well.

But Ackerman helped the team do better. "We got better every year I was there," she says. She scored 1,500 points in her four years at the school.

She had a great record. But still, Ackerman couldn't play pro ball in this country. There was no league to join.

So she went to France. There, she played one season of pro ball.

Then, she left the basketball court. And she went to a court of law. Ackerman went to law school. Later, she worked as a lawyer for the NBA.

She was soon promoted to special assistant to the NBA commissioner. That put her in position to make history.

How did Ackerman start the WNBA? First, she spoke to people at the NBA. She told them that fans would watch women play.

Next, she talked to big companies like Nike. They agreed to advertise during the games. Finally, she got ESPN on board. The top sports channel agreed to air many of the women's games.

In 1996, Ackerman's dream came true. The WNBA was created. And the rest is basketball history.

What advice would Ackerman give to young female athletes? She says to focus on school as well as sports. "Most of the players in the WNBA have their college degrees. And I'm very proud of that," she says.

How does Ackerman feel about her career? "I feel very privileged to be at the center of women's sports right now," she says. "It's a very exciting time. It's perhaps the most exciting time in our history."

Ackerman tells young athletes to focus on school. Why does she think that's important?

Time-out

with Teresa Weatherspoon of the
New York Liberty

It was Game 2 of the 1999 WNBA Championships. The New York Liberty were down by two points. If they lost this game, the Houston Comets would win the series.

Teresa Weatherspoon stepped in. She threw up a crazy shot. She was well behind the half-court line. It was amazing. The shot slid through the net.

The fans were shocked. The Comets couldn't believe it. Weatherspoon's teammates raced up to hug her. The Liberty had won the game!

That shot is just one reason Weatherspoon is a queen of the court.

But Weatherspoon is even better on defense. Twice, she's led the league in steals. She stalks her opponents while they dribble upcourt. A sudden flash of hands, and it's gone. Weatherspoon has the ball!

TERESA WEATHERSPOON

Stats compiled at end of 2001 season. © AP Photo/Kathy Willens.

Vital Stats

Born: 12/8/65
Height: 5′ 8″
College:
Louisiana Tech

Team:
New York Liberty
Playing Position:
Guard

Career Averages:
6.8 points
2.49 steals
6.3 assists

Carolyn Peck, General Manager
and Head Coach of the Orlando Miracle

Imagine starting your own basketball team. Does it sound like a dream? For Carolyn Peck, this is no dream. It's a reality.

Peck put together the Orlando Miracle. She's the team's general manager.

She also coaches the team. It's unusual to work as both general manager and head coach. It's a lot of work!

As the general manager, Peck chooses the new players. She also trades players. And she handles the team's business.

As the head coach, Peck helps the players work together to win. So, she is truly responsible for the team's success.

Carolyn Peck is no stranger to success. She started playing basketball as a young girl. She went on to play in college. In 1991, she joined a professional team in Japan.

Orlando Miracle general manager and head coach Carolyn Peck. She's at a practice at the Miracle's gym in Orlando, Florida. "I enjoy watching my team practice," Peck says.

Peck started coaching just two years later. Soon, she proved that she was a great coach. In 1999, she was named *Associated Press* Coach of the Year.

That's when Peck started with the Orlando Miracle. She knew it would be hard to put together a new team. But she had a good attitude.

"We are going to try to play as hard as we can," she said at the time. "None of these players has played on the same team before. But their strengths are showing."

Peck's own strengths are showing now. The team is improving. Plus, her players respect her.

"She's a player's coach," said former Miracle guard Adrienne Johnson. "Every player in the league wants to play for her. But when we're on the court, it's business."

Assistant coach Charlene Thomas-Swinson agrees that Peck is a tough coach. "She never loses that aggressiveness. That's what separates her from the rest."

Peck has advice for girls who want to play in the WNBA. She says it takes "a

determination to work hard." She also tells girls "to stay away from drugs and alcohol. And stay away from friends who might get you into trouble."

Peck adds, "Play as hard as you can in junior high and high school. Get a college degree. Then come to the WNBA!"

Peck loves her spot in the WNBA. "I enjoy watching my team practice every day," she said. "And with all the talent that's coming into the league, sorry, guys, but I have the best seat in the house!"

Which of Peck's jobs is more important—manager or coach? Why?

Time-out

Chamique "Meek" Holdsclaw is a winner!
Her high school team won four state titles. Her
college team, the University of Tennessee, won
three championships.

How good was she in college? They named
a road after her in Tennessee! That's why the
WNBA's Washington Mystics wanted her. She
was the No. 1 pick in the 1999 draft.

Growing up, Holdsclaw practiced a lot. "Big
boys, small boys, whomever. I was always
ready to take them on," she says. "I wasn't
scared of anybody's game."

In the WNBA, Holdsclaw won the rookie-
of-the-year award. And she's been selected to
play in three WNBA All-Star games.

Just ask Michael Jordan about her. "Meek
is fun to watch," he says. "She's exciting. She'll
definitely take women's sports to a new high."

CHAMIQUE HOLDSCLAW

Stats compiled at end of 2001 season. © AP Photo/Rick Bowmer.

Vital Stats

Born: 8/9/77

Height: 6′ 2″

College:
  Tennessee

Team:
  Washington Mystics

Playing Position:
  Forward

Career Averages:
  17.1 points
  8.1 rebounds
  2.4 assists

Lisa White, Trainer
for the New York Liberty

Some say basketball is not a contact sport. Tell that to the WNBA players!

Think about it. They bump for rebounds. They catch elbows. They dive for loose balls. And they don't wear pads.

That's why each WNBA team has an athletic trainer. The trainer helps players deal with the bumping and banging. The trainer for the New York Liberty is Lisa White.

White treats torn muscles. She also treats sprained ankles, bone bruises, and more. "Before practice, I treat injured players," says White. "We do exercises. We do stretching. I tape ankles and other body parts."

But it's not just the injured athletes who need White. She is also in charge of **conditioning** for every athlete.

White has a very important role on game

© AP Photo/Jeff Zelevansky

Trainer Lisa White *(right)* tends to Sue Wicks of the New York Liberty. Wicks was injured during a game against the Detroit Shock. They're at Madison Square Garden in New York City.

nights. She is always on guard. She needs to be ready if a player goes down.

When a player does get hurt, White acts fast. "First I ask them questions," she says. "That helps me find out where the injury is. I need to see if they can return to play."

Take, for example, one game in 1999. The New York Liberty were playing the Cleveland Rockers. It was just a minute into the game. Liberty superstar Rebecca Lobo went down. It was White's job to figure out what had happened. As it turned out, Lobo was seriously hurt. White kept her out of the game.

White's main goal is preventing injuries. "I try to prevent injuries by having players lift weights," she says. "I also teach good **nutrition**."

White has been with the Liberty since 1997. That was the first WNBA season. Growing up, she always loved sports. But she never thought she would end up working in the pros.

"I didn't really know what I wanted to do. Then I went to college. There, I learned about athletic training," White says.

In college, she studied **anatomy** and nutrition. Then, she did volunteer work. She spent 1,500 hours with a pro trainer. Finally, she got a degree in sports medicine.

After college, she worked as a trainer for a soccer team. But basketball was her first love. She was thrilled when she was offered a job for the Liberty.

White thinks her job is great. "I love being part of the team. I love working with athletes. I love helping them reach their goals."

And the players couldn't do it without her.

Say you're a reporter. What questions would you ask Lisa White about her job?

Time-out

with Ticha Penicheiro of the
Sacramento Monarchs

American women used to go to Europe to play pro ball. Now it's the other way around. The best Europeans are coming to play in the WNBA. The Sacramento Monarchs' Ticha Penicheiro is one example.

Penicheiro is from Portugal. And she just might be the world's best passer. She's the master of the "no-look" pass. She looks in one direction to fool the defender. But the ball is headed the other way.

Many of her passes end up as easy Monarchs baskets. Penicheiro leads the WNBA in assists.

Fans, coaches, and teammates are in awe of Penicheiro's talent. Says teammate Ruthie Bolton-Holifield, "She surprises us all the time! Even in practice, sometimes she'll pass. And we're all wondering, 'Ticha, where did *that* come from?'"

TICHA PENICHEIRO

Stats compiled at end of 2001 season. © AP Photo/Matt York.

Vital Stats

Born: 9/18/74
Height: 5' 11"
College:
Old Dominion

Team:
Sacramento Monarchs
Playing Position:
Guard

Career Averages:
6.8 points
2.12 steals
7.5 assists

Patty Broderick, Referee

Not long ago, many people thought women couldn't be good refs. They can't handle the pressure, critics said.

Patty Broderick has proven them wrong.

Broderick is a WNBA referee. It's her duty to **enforce** the rules. She calls the fouls. And she keeps the peace.

"I love it," says Broderick. "I love getting in the middle of things and getting my hands dirty."

Broderick discovered basketball as a kid in Indiana. She played basketball with her three brothers.

Broderick usually won. "No one ever made me feel like this was a boy's sport," she says. "I just thought I was supposed to play like everybody else."

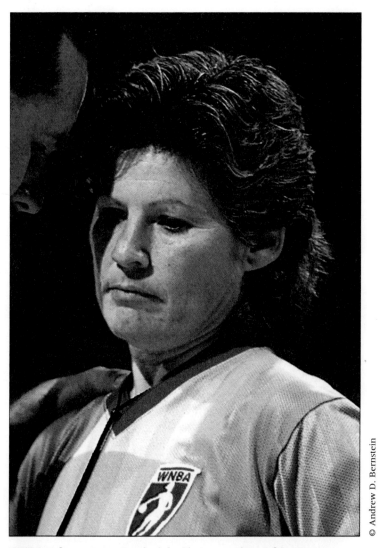

© Andrew D. Bernstein

WNBA referee Patty Broderick. She's meeting referee Jason Phillips at center court to discuss a call. "I love getting in the middle of things and getting my hands dirty," Broderick says.

Broderick played through high school. She didn't think she was good enough to play pro ball. But she wanted to stay in the game.

In her senior year, she started reffing a league of young girls. "I was hooked," Broderick says.

Broderick went from there to high school games. Then she reffed in college. And she reffed the 1996 Olympics. The next year, the WNBA was formed. They wanted the best female officials. So they called Broderick.

"The style of a WNBA game is incredible," Broderick says. "It's faster than college. And it's more athletic. I really have to stay on my toes."

A good ref has to be physically fit. "We are running after the best athletes in the world every night," Broderick says. "How are you going to do that if you're not in great shape?"

But the most important part of her job may be her people skills. Players can lose their tempers. They shout. They scream. And they get nasty. Sometimes their anger is directed at the refs.

That's when Broderick lays down the law.

"It's okay to question a call," she says. "But it's not okay to yell at me."

Most of the name-calling actually comes from the stands. "I've heard everything," laughs Broderick. "'Kill the ref!' 'Hey ref, you're blind.' The best one was, 'Hey, ref, go work at Foot Locker!'"

Some people might think that being a ref is a thankless job. But Broderick disagrees. "I travel. I stay in shape. I'm a big part of the sport. Who wouldn't love this job?" she says. "There are only two kinds of people on the court: the players and the refs. You can't start the game without either one."

How do you think Patty Broderick stays calm on the court?

Time-out

with Sheryl Swoopes of the Houston Comets

Who rules the WNBA court? It's the Houston Comets' Sheryl Swoopes.

Swoopes has done everything a basketball player can do. Her team won four straight championships. She's won the league scoring title. And she's won the best defensive player award. Plus, she's won the league's Most Valuable Player award. Wow!

Swoopes says playing in the WNBA is "a dream come true." What's left for her to achieve? Well, she could take on Michael Jordan in a game of one-on-one. Wait! She's already done that!

So, what does Swoopes do when she's not playing basketball? She likes to hang out with Jordan. No, not *Michael* Jordan. Swoopes's five-year-old son shares the superstar's name.

SHERYL SWOOPES

Stats compiled at end of 2001 season. © AP Photo/Tim Johnson.

Vital Stats

Born: 3/25/71
Height: 6′ 0″
College:
Texas Tech

Team:
Houston Comets
Playing Position:
Forward

Career Averages:
17.3 points
5.6 rebounds
2.4 steals

Alicia Parker, Director of Security

She's a WNBA player. But not the kind of player you think.

She doesn't score points. She doesn't dribble. She doesn't block shots.

Her season lasts 12 months and not three. And she has to be on top of her game all the time.

Her name is Alicia Parker. She's the head of security for the WNBA.

That means she's in charge of safety. She protects the players, the coaches, and others.

"It's a fulfilling job and one that I love," says Parker. That's why she's been with the WNBA since its first season in 1997.

Parker may love her job. But it isn't always easy. Some nights there are games in eight arenas. Parker has to make sure that each game runs smoothly.

Alicia Parker, director of security for the WNBA. "I get to meet all of the players," Parker says. To prove it, she's standing with *(back row, from left)*: Natalie Williams of the Utah Starzz, Chamique Holdsclaw of the Washington Mystics, and Lisa Leslie of the Los Angeles Sparks. In the front is Shannon Johnson of the Orlando Miracle.

How does she do that? She stays in close touch with security officers at each game. "They are my eyes and ears at the arena," Parker explains.

"I make sure they're in position during games," she says.

Parker has other duties, too. She talks to the players about safety. She tells them how to be safe both on and off the court.

"I get to meet all of the players in the WNBA," says Parker. "I speak to the players before the season starts. I talk to them about staying safe, whether it's at home or traveling."

Parker also speaks to players about the dangers of alcohol and drugs.

"I'm someone the players can turn to during the season and also during the off-season," says Parker. "I'm here at all times for our players."

But sometimes Parker has to be tough. Sometimes she has to talk to players who have stepped out of line.

If a player breaks a rule, she hears from Parker. If a player speaks out against an official, she hears from Parker. And it's usually bad news.

Sports reporter Kristie Ackert. She's standing in front of Madison Square Garden, home of the New York Liberty. Covering a game, Ackert says, "is always exciting."

the team is practicing a new play. Maybe a player is shooting really well. Maybe another player has been hurt.

Ackert will put these details in her article. Her articles don't just report the final score. She wants her articles to tell a story that fans might not know.

In the afternoon, Ackert takes a break. Then she returns to the Garden for the game. She sits close to the action. She sees every fast break. She follows every foul. She hears the squeak of each sneaker.

On game day, Ackert often writes two stories. Her first article is due as soon as the game ends. It will be printed in an early **edition** of the newspaper. "The pressure is intense. But I love the feeling," says Ackert.

Ackert's second article will be printed in a late edition of the paper. It will be more detailed than the first. She doesn't have much time to write this story. So, after the game, she hurries to the locker room. She needs to get comments from the team.

"I hear the coaches talk about the game,"

says Ackert. "I talk to the players. Then I begin writing. I have to make my deadline."

The women players she writes about are pioneers. And Ackert is a pioneer, too. Not many sportswriters are women.

"I have a few women sportswriting friends," Ackert says. "There are not a lot of us. But that's changing."

Ackert worked hard to become a great writer. And she loves her job. "I love the way that my job changes every day," she says. "I like being where things happen."

Ackert tells students that being a journalist is great. "Go ahead and do it!" she says. "It's always exciting and a lot of fun."

What are some advantages to being a pioneer in a field? What are some disadvantages?

Glossary

anatomy *(noun)* the study of the structure of the human body

charity *(noun)* an organization that raises money to help people in need

conditioning *(noun)* exercise or physical training

determination *(noun)* the quality of being firm in a decision

easygoing *(adjective)* relaxed or friendly

edition *(noun)* a version of a newspaper. (Some newspapers are printed more than once a day.)

enforce *(verb)* to make sure that a rule is followed

nutrition *(noun)* what you eat

opportunity *(noun)* a chance to do something

pioneer *(noun)* one of the first people to work in a new area